Vegetarian Mediterranean Cookbook

Over 50 recipes for appetizers, salads, dips, and main dishes

By Susan Evans

D1642834

Other popular books by Susan Evans

Quick & Easy Asian Vegetarian Cookbook:
Over 50 recipes for stir fries, rice, noodles, and appetizers

Vegetarian Slow Cooker Cookbook:
Over 75 recipes for meals, soups, stews, desserts, and sides

Quick & Easy Vegetarian Rice Cooker Meals:
Over 50 recipes for breakfast, main dishes, and desserts

Quick & Easy Vegan Desserts Cookbook:
Over 80 delicious recipes for cakes, cupcakes, brownies, cookies, fudge,
pies, candy, and so much more!

Quick & Easy Rice Cooker Meals:
Over 60 recipes for breakfast, main dishes, soups, and desserts

Quick & Easy Microwave Meals:
Over 50 recipes for breakfast, snacks, meals and desserts

Halloween Cookbook:
80 Ghoulish recipes for appetizers, meals, drinks, and desserts

FREE BONUS!

Would you like to receive one of my cookbooks for free? Just leave me on honest review on Amazon and I will send you a digital version of the cookbook of your choice! All you have to do is email me proof of your review and the desired cookbook and format to susan.evans.author@gmail.com. Thank you for your support, and have fun cooking!

INTRODUCTION

The Mediterranean diet has long been recognized as one of the healthiest on Earth. The largely plant-based diet mainly consists of olive oil, legumes, unrefined cereals, fruits, and vegetables. Due to the disease-fighting antioxidants and phytonutrients, it has been found to lower the risk of cardiovascular disease, cancer, diabetes, and has been shown to be a great way to manage your weight. Just as important, Mediterranean meals taste delicious!

Transition into a Mediterranean diet with mouthwatering and simple to follow vegetable-based recipes. Whether you are looking to enhance your health and wellbeing, or just want to create some tasty and easy meals for you and your loved ones, you will find everything you need in the following flavorful and wholesome recipes. From appetizers, salads, hummus, dips, and main dishes, you are sure to find a great meal that even non-vegetarians will enjoy. Let's get cooking!

MEASUREMENT CONVERSIONS

Liquid/Volume Measurements (approximate)

1 teaspoon = 1/6 fluid ounce (oz.) = 1/3 tablespoon = 5 ml

1 tablespoon = 1/2 fluid ounce (oz.) = 3 teaspoons = 15 ml

1 fluid ounce (oz.) = 2 tablespoons = 1/8 cup = 30 ml

1/4 cup = 2 fluid ounces (oz.) = 4 tablespoons = 60 ml

1/3 cup = 2⅔ fluid ounces (oz.) = 5 ⅓ tablespoons = 80 ml

1/2 cup = 4 fluid ounces (oz.) = 8 tablespoons = 120 ml

2/3 cup = 5⅓ fluid ounces (oz.) = 10⅔ tablespoons = 160 ml

3/4 cup = 6 fluid ounces (oz.) = 12 tablespoons = 180 ml

7/8 cup = 7 fluid ounces (oz.) = 14 tablespoons = 210 ml

1 cup = 8 fluid ounces (oz.) = 1/2 pint = 240 ml

1 pint = 16 fluid ounces (oz.) = 2 cups = 1/2 quart = 475 ml

1 quart = 4 cups = 32 fluid ounces (oz.) = 2 pints = 950 ml

1 liter = 1.055 quarts = 4.22 cups = 2.11 pints = 1000 ml

1 gallon = 4 quarts = 8 pints = 3.8 liters

Dry/Weight Measurements (approximate)

1 ounce (oz.) = 30 grams (g)

2 ounces (oz.) = 55 grams (g)

3 ounces (oz.) = 85 grams (g)

1/4 pound (lb.) = 4 ounces (oz.) = 125 grams (g)

1/2 pound (lb.) = 8 ounces (oz.) = 240 grams (g)

3/4 pound (lb.) = 12 ounces (oz.) = 375 grams (g)

1 pound (lb.) = 16 ounces (oz.) = 455 grams (g)

2 pounds (lbs.) = 32 ounces (oz.) = 910 grams (g)

1 kilogram (kg) = 2.2 pounds (lbs.) = 1000 gram (g)

APPETIZERS

Greek Lentil Soup

SERVINGS: 4
PREP TIME: 20 min.
TOTAL TIME: 1 hour 20 min

Ingredients

- 8 ounces brown lentils
- 1/4 cup olive oil
- 1 tablespoon minced garlic
- 1 onion, minced
- 1 large carrot, chopped
- 1 quart water
- 1 pinch dried oregano
- 1 pinch crushed dried rosemary
- 2 bay leaves
- 1 tablespoon tomato paste
- salt and ground black pepper, to taste
- 1 teaspoon olive oil, or to taste
- 1 teaspoon red wine vinegar, to taste

Instructions

1. Place lentils in a large saucepan. Add enough water to cover lentils by an inch. Bring water to a boil and cook about 10 minutes or until tender. Drain.
2. Heat olive oil in a saucepan over medium heat. Add garlic, onion, and carrot. Cook and stir about 5 minutes or until the onion has softened and turned translucent. Pour in lentils, 1 quart water, oregano, rosemary, and bay leaves. Bring to a boil and then reduce heat to medium-low. Cover and simmer for 10 minutes.
3. Stir in tomato paste and season with salt and pepper. Cover and simmer 30 to 40 minutes or until the lentils have softened, occasionally stirring. Add additional water if the soup becomes too thick. Drizzle with 1 teaspoon olive oil and red wine vinegar to taste.

Braised Baby Artichokes

SERVINGS: 6
PREP TIME: 10 min.
TOTAL TIME: 30 min.

Ingredients

- 6 tablespoons olive oil
- 2 lbs. baby artichokes, trimmed
- 1/2 cup lemon juice
- 4 cloves garlic, thinly sliced
- 1/2 teaspoon salt
- 1 1/2 lb. tomatoes, seeded and diced
- 1/2 cup sliced toasted almonds

Instructions

1. In skillet over medium heat, cook oil, and add artichokes. When artichokes begin to sizzle, add lemon juice and garlic, seasoning with salt. Reduce heat to medium-low, cover, and simmer for 15 minutes.
2. Uncover pan and add tomatoes. Simmer 5 to 10 minutes, or until most of liquid has evaporated and mixture thickens. Season with salt and pepper, sprinkling with toasted almonds.
3. Serve warm.

Chickpea Croquettes

SERVINGS: 6
PREP/ TOTAL TIME: 20 min.

Ingredients

- 2 (14 oz.) cans chickpeas, rinsed and drained
- 1/2 cup breadcrumbs
- 1/4 cup olive oil
- 8 sun-dried tomatoes (2 oz.) packed in oil, drained and finely chopped
- 2 tablespoons sumac, if desired
- 1 tablespoon ground coriander
- 1 tablespoon ground cumin
- 3 cloves garlic (1 tablespoon), minced
- 1/2 cup all-purpose flour
- 2 tablespoon canola oil

Instructions

1. In a blender or food processor, pulse chickpeas, breadcrumbs, olive oil, tomatoes, sumac, coriander, cumin, and garlic until puréed. Season with salt and pepper, to taste.
2. Roll mixture and form walnut-sized patties, approximately 18 medium-size croquettes or 24 small croquettes. Dig the croquettes in flour, and shake off excess.
3. In a skillet over medium-low heat, cook oil and add half of the croquettes. Cook for 2 minutes on each side, or until brown. Repeat with the rest of the croquettes.

Hazelnut Cinnamon Biscotti

SERVINGS: 30
PREP TIME: 20 min.
TOTAL TIME: 1 hour

Ingredients

- 3/4 cup butter
- 1 cup white sugar
- 2 eggs
- 1 1/2 teaspoons vanilla extract
- 2 1/2 cups all-purpose flour
- 1 teaspoon ground cinnamon
- 3/4 teaspoon baking powder
- 1/2 teaspoon salt
- 1 cup hazelnuts

Instructions

1. Preheat oven to 350°F (175°C). Grease a cookie sheet or line with parchment paper.
2. Combine butter and sugar in a medium bowl until light and fluffy. Beat in eggs and vanilla. Sift together the flour, cinnamon, baking powder, and salt, and mix into egg mixture. Stir in hazelnuts. Shape dough into two equal logs 12 inches long. Place on baking sheet, and flatten to 1/2 inch thickness.
3. Bake for 30 minutes in preheated oven or until edges are golden and center is firm. Remove from oven to cool.
4. Slice the loaves diagonally into 1/2 inch thick slices. Return to the baking sheet. Bake for another 10 minutes and turn over once.
5. Cool and store in an airtight container at room temperature.

Chimichurri Avocado Bruschetta

SERVINGS: 6
PREP/ TOTAL TIME: 20 min.

Ingredients

- 2 tablespoons lemon juice
- 2 tablespoons red wine vinegar
- 3 cloves garlic (1 tablespoon), minced
- 3/4 teaspoon salt
- 1/2 teaspoon red pepper flakes
- 1/2 teaspoon dried oregano
- 1/4 teaspoon ground black pepper
- 1/4 cup olive oil
- 1/4 cup chopped cilantro
- 1/4 cup chopped fresh parsley
- 2 avocados, peeled, pitted, and cubed
- 6 1/2-inch-thick slices of whole-grain or ciabatta bread, toasted

Instructions

1. In small bowl, combine lemon juice, vinegar, garlic, salt, red pepper flakes, oregano, and black pepper.
2. Whisk in oil; stir in cilantro and parsley. Gently combine avocado cubes.
3. Spoon mixture onto toast slices. Serve.

Olives and Cheesy Cracker Bread

SERVINGS: 16
PREP TIME: 5 min.
TOTAL TIME: 15 min.

Ingredients

- 1 cracker bread (from 15 3/4-oz package), about 12 inches in diameter
- 1 1/2 cups (6 oz.) shredded Italian cheese blend
- 1/3 cup pitted Kalamata olives, cut in half
- 1 tablespoon chopped fresh basil leaves

Instructions

1. Preheat oven to 375°F (190°C).
1. Place cracker bread on large cookie sheet and sprinkle cheese and olives on top.
2. Bake 4 to 6 minutes, or until cheese is melted.
3. Top with basil and break cracker bread into small pieces, or cut into 3-inch squares.
4. Serve warm.

Zucchini Bites

SERVINGS: 6
PREP/ TOTAL TIME: 45 min.

Ingredients

- 1 (8 ounce) brick feta cheese
- 2 tablespoons whipped cream cheese
- 1/2 teaspoon lemon zest, freshly grated
- 1/2 teaspoon oregano
- 1/2 teaspoon cilantro
- 1/2 teaspoon paprika
- 1/4 teaspoon garlic powder
- 1/8 teaspoon cayenne pepper
- 3 medium zucchini, ends trimmed and sliced
- 1/8 of an inch thick
- 1 teaspoon olive oil

Instructions

1. Crumble the feta in a food processor or blender. Add cream cheese and process for 3 to 4 minutes, or until smooth, making sure to scrape down the sides.
2. In a medium bowl, transfer the mix and add lemon zest, oregano, cilantro, paprika, garlic powder and cayenne. Combine and stir well.
3. Refrigerate and cover at least 30 minutes.
4. Place the zucchini slices in a bowl and drizzle with olive oil. Gently toss to coat.
5. Heat a grill pan over medium heat and grill the zucchini slices for about 2 to 3 minutes. Flip and grill another 1 to 2 minutes on the second side. Transfer grilled slices to a wire rack to cool.
6. Thinly spread the whipped feta mixture onto zucchini slices.
7. Start at the widest end and roll each slice.
8. Serve.

Tomato and Tapenade Tartlet Pastries

SERVINGS: 6
PREP TIME: 10 min.
TOTAL TIME: 30 min.

Ingredients

- 2 cups cherry tomatoes, halved
- 1 teaspoon olive oil
- 1/4 teaspoon herbs de Provence
- 1/2 (17.3-oz.) package puff pastry, thawed
- 6 teaspoon black olive tapenade
- 9 teaspoon prepared hummus

Instructions

1. Preheat oven to 425°F (220°C). Spray baking sheet with cooking spray or line with parchment paper.
2. In a small bowl, toss cherry tomatoes with oil and herbs de Provence. Season with salt and pepper. Set aside.
3. Cut puff pastry into six 3 1/2-inch rounds, and transfer to prepared baking sheet. Puncture holes with fork.
4. Spread each puff pastry round with 1 teaspoon tapenade and 1 1/2 teaspoon hummus. Top with 8 cherry tomato halves.
5. Bake for 20 minutes or until crusts are browned on bottom and edges.
6. Serve warm.

SALADS

Roasted Summer Vegetables and Quinoa Salad

SERVINGS: 4
PREP TIME: 15 min.
TOTAL TIME: 1 hour 20 min.

Ingredients

- 1/3 cup uncooked quinoa, rinsed (or 1 cup cooked quinoa)
- 1 small eggplant (about 3/4 pound), diced
- 1 small zucchini, diced
- 1 small yellow squash (or another zucchini), diced
- 3 to 4 tablespoons olive oil, divided
- Salt and freshly ground black pepper
- 1 1/2 to 2 tablespoons lemon juice, about 1 medium lemon
- 1 clove garlic, pressed or minced
- 1/2 cup halved grape tomatoes
- 2 tablespoons chopped fresh basil leaves
- 2 tablespoons chopped fresh mint leaves
- 2 tablespoons pine nuts, toasted
- Crumbled feta, optional

Instructions

1. Preheat oven to 425°F (220°C) with racks in the upper and lower thirds of oven. Line two large rimmed baking sheets with parchment paper.
2. Divide eggplant, zucchini and yellow squash between the two baking sheets. Drizzle with 1 tablespoon olive oil and toss. Sprinkle salt and pepper. Roast about 20 to 30 minutes or until vegetables are soft and a bit brown. Set vegetables aside to cool.
3. In a small saucepan, combine the uncooked quinoa with 2/3 cup water. Bring to boil over medium-high heat, cover, and reduce to low heat. Simmer about 15 minutes or until water is absorbed. Remove from heat and let quinoa steam for 5 minutes with lid on. Remove lid, fluff quinoa with a fork, and set aside.

4. Cook pine nuts in a small skillet over medium heat stirring frequently, about 5 to 10 minutes, or until lightly gold and fragrant. Transfer to a bowl and allow to cool.
5. Whisk the lemon juice and garlic together in a large serving bowl. Slowly pour in remaining 2 tablespoons of olive oil while whisking constantly. Add tomatoes, quinoa, basil, mint, roasted vegetables, and pine nuts, gently stirring to combine. Season with salt, pepper and maybe a bit of lemon juice, to taste. Garnish with crumbled feta, if desired.
6. Serve at room temperature or store in an airtight container for up to 3 days in the refrigerator.

Insalata Caprese

SERVINGS: 6
PREP/ TOTAL TIME: 15 min.

Ingredients

- 4 large ripe tomatoes, sliced
- 1/4 inch thick Tomatoes
- 1 pound fresh mozzarella cheese, sliced
- 1/4 inch thick
- 1/3 cup fresh basil leaves
- 3 tablespoons extra virgin olive oil
- fine sea salt, to taste
- ground black pepper, to taste

Instructions

1. On a large platter, overlap and alternate tomato slices, mozzarella cheese slices, and basil leaves.
2. Drizzle with olive oil.
3. Season with sea salt and pepper.

Grapes, Feta, and Mint Lentil Salad

SERVINGS: 4
PREP TIME: 10 min.
TOTAL TIME: 20 min.

Ingredients

- 3 tablespoons olive oil
- 2 leeks (1 3/4 cups), white and light green parts thinly sliced
- 2 tablespoons sherry vinegar
- 2 teaspoon whole-grain mustard
- 1 (17.6 oz.) pkg. cooked lentils, gently broken apart, or 2 cups cooked lentil
- 1 1/2 cups red grapes, halved
- 1/4 cup chopped roasted pistachios
- 3 tablespoons finely chopped mint
- 3 tablespoons finely chopped parsley
- 1/4 cup crumbled feta

Instructions

1. In a skillet, heat oil over medium heat. Add leeks, stir often and cook 7 to 9 minutes or until tender and translucent. Remove from heat, and stir in sherry vinegar and mustard.
2. In large bowl, combine lentils, leek mixture, grapes, pistachios, mint, and parsley. Season with salt and pepper and top with crumbled feta.

Healthy Greek Salad

SERVINGS: 6
PREP/ TOTAL TIME: 15 min.

Ingredients

- 3 large ripe tomatoes, chopped
- 2 cucumbers, peeled and chopped
- 1 small red onion, chopped
- 1/4 cup olive oil
- 4 teaspoons lemon juice
- 1 1/2 teaspoons dried oregano
- salt and pepper, to taste
- 1 cup crumbled feta cheese
- 6 black Greek olives, pitted and sliced

Instructions

1. In a salad bowl or serving platter, combine tomatoes, cucumber, and onion.
2. Sprinkle with oil, lemon juice, oregano, and salt and pepper; to taste. Top with feta cheese and olives.
3. Serve.

Quick and Easy Arugula Salad

SERVINGS: 4
PREP/ TOTAL TIME: 15 min.

Ingredients

- 4 cups young arugula leaves, rinsed and dried
- 1 cup cherry tomatoes, halved
- 1/4 cup pine nuts
- 2 tablespoons grapeseed oil or olive oil
- 1 tablespoon rice vinegar
- Salt, to taste
- freshly ground black pepper to taste
- 1/4 cup grated Parmesan cheese
- 1 large avocado, peeled, pitted and sliced

Instructions

1. In a large plastic bowl, combine arugula, cherry tomatoes, pine nuts, oil, vinegar, and Parmesan cheese. Season with salt and pepper to taste. Cover and shake to mix.
2. Divide onto plates, and top with avocado slices.

Mediterranean Kale

SERVINGS: 6
PREP TIME: 15 min.
TOTAL TIME: 25 min.

Ingredients

- 12 cups chopped kale
- 2 tablespoons lemon juice
- 1 tablespoon olive oil
- 1 tablespoon minced garlic
- 1 teaspoon soy sauce
- salt and ground pepper to taste

Instructions

1. Place a steamer insert in a saucepan, filling with water just below the bottom of steamer. Cover and over high heat bring water to a boil. Add kale, cover, and steam 7 to 10 minutes or until just tender.
2. Whisk the lemon juice, olive oil, garlic, soy sauce, salt, and black pepper in a large bowl.
3. Toss kale into dressing until well coated. Serve.

Barley Salad

SERVINGS: 6
PREP TIME: 15 min.
TOTAL TIME: 45 min.

Ingredients

- 1 cup barley
- 2 1/2 cups water
- 7 sun-dried tomatoes
- 2 cloves garlic
- 2 tablespoons olive oil
- 1 tablespoon balsamic vinegar
- 1/2 cup finely chopped cilantro
- 1 (4 ounce) can chopped black olives
- 2 tablespoons olive oil

Instructions

1. In a saucepan over high heat, bring barley and water to a boil. Reduce heat to medium-low, cover, and simmer about 30 minutes or until barley is tender, but slightly firm in center. Drain and cool in a separate bowl.
2. In a blender, puree sun-dried tomatoes, garlic, 2 tablespoons olive oil, and balsamic vinegar, until smooth. Pour mixture over the barley. Gently mix in the cilantro, olives, and remaining olive oil. Cover, and refrigerate.
3. Stir before serving.

Mediterranean Greek Salad

SERVINGS: 8
PREP/ TOTAL TIME: 15 min.

Ingredients

- 3 cucumbers, seeded and sliced
- 1 1/2 cups crumbled feta cheese
- 1 cup black olives, pitted and sliced
- 3 cups diced Roma tomatoes
- 1/3 cup diced oil packed sun-dried tomatoes, drained, reserve oil
- 1/2 red onion, sliced

Instructions

1. Combine cucumbers, feta cheese, olives, Roma tomatoes, sun-dried tomatoes, 2 tablespoons reserved sun-dried tomato oil, and red onion in a large salad bowl. Toss.
2. Chill and serve.

Rocket and Veggie Ham Salad

SERVINGS: 2
PREP/ TOTAL TIME: 5 min.

Ingredients

- 1 (7 ounce) bag arugula
- 7 ounces of your favorite vegetarian ham deli slices, torn into thin strips
- 1/4 cup olive oil
- 1/4 cup balsamic vinegar

Instructions

1. Place arugula on a large flat platter.
2. Top with ham.
3. Drizzle olive oil and balsamic vinegar on top.

HUMMUS AND DIPS

Black Bean Hummus

SERVINGS: 8
PREP/ TOTAL TIME: 10 min.

Ingredients

- 1 clove garlic
- 1 (15 ounce) can black beans, drain and reserve liquid
- 2 tablespoons lemon juice
- 1 1/2 tablespoons tahini
- 3/4 teaspoon ground cumin
- 1/2 teaspoon salt
- 1/4 teaspoon cayenne pepper
- 1/4 teaspoon paprika
- 10 Greek olives

Instructions

1. Mince garlic in a food processor or blender. Add black beans, 2 tablespoons of reserved liquid, lemon juice, tahini, 1/2 teaspoon cumin, 1/2 teaspoon salt, and 1/8 teaspoon cayenne pepper. Process until smooth.
2. Add additional seasoning and reserve liquid to taste.
3. Garnish with paprika and Greek olives.

Roasted Garlic Hummus

SERVINGS: 3
PREP/ TOTAL TIME: 1 hour

Ingredients

- 4–5 heads of garlic
- 1 tablespoon plus1/4 cup olive oil, divided
- 1 (28 oz.) can chickpeas, rinsed and drained
- 1/2 cup lemon juice
- 3 tablespoons tahini

Instructions

1. Preheat oven to 350°F (175°C). Cut tops off garlic heads, place on large sheet of aluminum foil, and drizzle with 1 tablespoon of olive oil. Wrap garlic heads tightly in the foil, and bake 30 to 45 minutes, or until soft. Let cool in foil.
2. In a blender or food processor, purée chickpeas for 1 minute, or until finely chopped. Add lemon juice, 1/4 cup olive oil, tahini, and 1/2 cup water. Blend mixture for 2 to 3 minutes, or until smooth.
3. Squeeze out the roasted garlic pulp from each clove in the chickpea mixture. Pulse hummus a few times to combine. Season with salt and pepper.
4. Spread in thin layer on large plate, and drizzle with olive oil. Serve with pita wedges.

Delightfully Good Hummus

Ingredients

- 1 garlic clove
- 1 (19 ounce) can garbanzo beans (chickpeas), half the liquid reserved
- 4 tablespoons lemon juice
- 2 tablespoons tahini
- 1 garlic clove, chopped
- 1 teaspoon salt black pepper
- 2 tablespoons olive oil

Instructions

1. Pour garbanzo beans (chickpeas) into a blender, and reserve a tablespoon for garnish. Place garlic, lemon juice, tahini, chopped garlic, and salt in a blender. Process until creamy.
2. Transfer mixture to a medium serving bowl and sprinkle with pepper. Pour olive oil on top.
3. Garnish with reserved chickpeas.

Tomato-Mint Salsa and Hummus Dip

SERVINGS: 8
PREP/TOTAL TIME: 10 min.

Ingredients

- 2 (1 1/2 cups) medium tomatoes, diced
- 1/4 cup diced white onion
- 2 tablespoons olive oil
- 2 tablespoons chopped fresh mint
- 1 1/2 tablespoons lemon juice
- 1 large package of your favorite Hummus

Instructions

1. Stir together tomatoes, diced onion, oil, mint, and lemon juice in small bowl. Season with salt and pepper. Let stand 5 minutes.
2. Spread Hummus in shallow dish and place salsa in center.

Sweet and Spicy Roasted Red Pepper Hummus

SERVINGS: 8
PREP/TOTAL TIME: 10 min.

Ingredients

- 1 (15 ounce) can garbanzo (chickpeas) beans, drained
- 1 (4 ounce) jar roasted red peppers
- 3 tablespoons lemon juice
- 1 1/2 tablespoons tahini
- 1 clove garlic, minced
- 1/2 teaspoon ground cumin
- 1/2 teaspoon cayenne pepper
- 1/4 teaspoon salt
- 1 tablespoon chopped fresh parsley

Instructions

1. Puree chickpeas, red peppers, lemon juice, tahini, garlic, cumin, cayenne, and salt in an electric blender or food processor. Process using long pulses until smooth and slightly fluffy. Scrape the mixture off the sides between pulses. Transfer to a serving bowl and refrigerate at least an hour.
2. Return to room temperature before serving. Sprinkle with the chopped parsley before serving.

Quince Paste

SERVINGS: 32
PREP TIME: 20 min.
TOTAL TIME: 4 hours

Ingredients

- 4 1/2 pounds ripe quinces
- 5 1/2 cups white sugar
- water to cover

Instructions

1. Wash, peel, and core the quinces. Reserve the cores and peels. Coarsely chop the quinces flesh and transfer to a large pan. Wrap cores and peels in cheesecloth, tie with kitchen string, and add it to the pan.
2. Pour in enough water to cover and boil half-covered, for 30 to 40 minutes or until the fruit is soft. Remove peel bag and sieve the quince flesh.
3. Transfer the quince pulp to a saucepan and add the sugar. Cook and stir over low heat until the sugar dissolves. Cook for about 1 1/2 hours. Stir frequently with a wooden spoon until the paste is thick with a deep orange color. Pull the spoon along the bottom of saucepan; the quince should stick to the spoon and leave a trail.
4. Lightly grease a 9x13 inch baking dish or line with parchment paper. Transfer the paste and spread about 1 1/2-inch thick. Smooth the top and cool.
5. Dry the paste for about 1 1/2 hours on the lowest oven setting, no higher than 125°F (52°C). Allow to cool before slicing. You can also use the traditional method of drying the paste for about 7 days.
6. Store in an airtight container in the refrigerator.

Quick and Easy Hummus

SERVINGS: 4
PREP/ TOTAL TIME: 5 min.

Ingredients

- 1 (15 ounce) can garbanzo beans (chickpeas), drained, liquid reserved
- 1 clove garlic, crushed
- 2 teaspoons ground cumin
- 1/2 teaspoon salt
- 1 tablespoon olive oil

Instructions

1. Combine all ingredients in a food processor or blender.
2. Blend on low speed, gradually adding reserved bean liquid, until desired consistency.

Roasted Pepper and Bean Dip

SERVINGS: 8
PREP/ TOTAL TIME: 15 min.

Ingredients

- 1/4 cup chopped fresh basil
- 1 teaspoon balsamic vinegar
- 1 (16 ounce) can cannellini beans, rinsed and drained
- 1 (7 ounce) bottle roasted red bell peppers, rinsed and drained
- 1 large garlic clove
- 2 tablespoons extra virgin olive oil
- 1/2 teaspoon salt
- 1/2 teaspoon freshly ground black pepper

Instructions

1. In a food processor or blender, place first five ingredients and process until smooth. While the processor is on, slowly add oil. Stir in salt and black pepper.
2. Serve or refrigerate.

MAIN DISHES

Orange Israeli Couscous with Raisins and Carrots

SERVINGS: 6
PREP TIME: 5 min.
TOTAL TIME: 30 min.

Ingredients

- 1 1/3 cups Israeli couscous
- 1 cup and 1 tablespoon no-pulp orange juice
- 1 cup water
- 3 medium carrots, grated (1 1/2 cups)
- 1/2 cup raisins
- 1 teaspoon ground cumin

Instructions

1. Spray medium saucepan with cooking spray. Add couscous, and heat over medium heat for 4 minutes, stirring frequently, until lightly browned.
2. Add 1 cup orange juice and 1 cup water to the saucepan; season with salt and pepper. Bring to a boil. Reduce heat to low. Cover and simmer for 12 minutes, or until liquid has absorbed. Remove from heat and cover for 5 minutes.
3. Stir in the remaining orange juice, carrots, raisins, and cumin.
4. Serve warm.

Baked Falafel

SERVINGS: 2
PREP TIME: 10 min.
TOTAL TIME: 30 min.

Ingredients

- 1/4 cup chopped onion
- 1 (15 ounce) can garbanzo beans (chickpeas), rinsed and drained
- 1/4 cup chopped fresh parsley
- 3 cloves garlic, minced
- 1 teaspoon ground cumin
- 1/4 teaspoon ground coriander
- 1/4 teaspoon salt
- 1/4 teaspoon baking soda
- 1 tablespoon all-purpose flour
- 1 egg, beaten
- 2 teaspoons olive oil

Instructions

1. Preheat an oven to 400°F (200°C).
2. Wrap onion in cheese cloth and squeeze out moisture. Set aside.
3. In a food processor, puree garbanzo beans (chickpeas), parsley, garlic, cumin, coriander, salt, and baking soda.
4. In a bowl, mix garbanzo bean mixture and onion together. Add and stir flour and egg. Shape mixture into four large patties and let stand for 15 minutes.
5. Heat olive oil in a large oven-safe skillet over medium-high heat. Place in patties in the skillet and cook about 3 minutes on each side or until golden brown. Transfer to the preheated oven and bake about 10 minutes or until heated through.

Feta and Spinach Pita Bake

SERVINGS: 6
PREP TIME: 10 min.
TOTAL TIME: 25 min.

Ingredients

- 1 (6 ounce) jar sun-dried tomato pesto
- 6 (6 inch) whole wheat pita breads
- 2 Roma (plum) tomatoes, chopped
- 1 bunch of spinach, rinsed and chopped
- 4 fresh mushrooms, sliced
- 1/2 cup crumbled feta cheese
- 2 tablespoons grated Parmesan cheese
- 3 tablespoons olive oil
- ground black pepper, to taste

Instructions

1. Preheat the oven to 350°F (175°C).
2. Spread pesto on one side of each pita bread. Place pita bread pesto-side up on a baking sheet. Top with tomatoes, spinach, mushrooms, feta cheese, and Parmesan cheese. Drizzle olive oil and season with pepper.
3. Bake in oven about 12 minutes or until pita breads are crisp.
4. Cut pitas into quarters and serve.

Tomatoes and White Beans Greek Pasta

SERVINGS: 4
PREP TIME: 10 min.
TOTAL TIME: 25 min.

Ingredients

- 8 ounces penne pasta
- 2 (14.5 ounce) cans Italian-style diced tomatoes
- 1 (19 ounce) can cannellini beans, drained and rinsed
- 10 ounces fresh spinach, washed and chopped
- 1/2 cup crumbled feta cheese

Instructions

1. Cook pasta in a large boiling pot of salted water until al dente.
2. In a large non-stick skillet, combine tomatoes and beans and bring to a boil over medium high heat. Reduce heat and simmer 10 minutes.
3. Add spinach to the sauce, and cook for 2 minutes or until spinach wilts, while constantly stirring.
4. Serve sauce over pasta. Sprinkle with feta.

Eggplant and Chickpea Stew

SERVINGS: 4
PREP TIME: 15 min.
TOTAL TIME: 45 min.

Ingredients

- 2/3 cup diced yellow onions
- 2/3 cup diced green bell peppers
- 1 1/2 teaspoons olive oil
- 1 cup cubed Asian eggplant (1-inch cubes)
- 1 tablespoon minced garlic
- 1 can (15 ounces) chickpeas, drained and rinsed
- 1 can (14 ounces) diced tomatoes
- 1 1/2 cups filtered water
- 1 cup fresh or frozen cut green beans
- 1/4 cup chopped fresh parslcy
- 1 teaspoon dried basil
- 1 teaspoon dried oregano
- 1 teaspoon curry powder
- 1 teaspoon sea salt
- 1/2 teaspoon freshly ground black pepper

Instructions

1. Place onions, bell peppers, and olive oil in a large pot. Cook and stir over medium heat for 2 to 3 minutes until softened. Add eggplant and garlic. Cook and stir for 2 minutes.
2. Add and stir in the remaining ingredients. Cover, reduce the heat to low, and simmer for 20 to 25 minutes or until the vegetables are tender. Add seasonings as desired.
3. Serve hot.

Curried Chickpea and Vegetable Stew with Lemon Couscous

SERVINGS: 5
PREP TIME: 15 min.
TOTAL TIME: 45 min.

Ingredients

- 2 cups onion, diced
- 1 cup green bell pepper, seeds and ribs removed, and diced
- 1 cup red bell pepper, seeds and ribs removed, and diced
- 1 tablespoon olive oil
- 2 tablespoons garlic, minced
- 2 teaspoons curry powder
- 2 teaspoons ground cumin
- 1 teaspoon ground coriander
- 1/2 teaspoon ground cinnamon
- 3 teaspoons sea salt
- 1 teaspoon freshly ground black pepper
- 3 cups sweet potato, diced
- 2 cups zucchini, quartered lengthwise and sliced
- 1 can (15 ounces) chickpeas, drained and rinsed
- 1 can (14.5 ounces) diced tomatoes
- 5 cups vegetable stock or 5 cups vegetable broth made from vegetable broth powder
- 6 tablespoons fresh or bottled lemon juice
- 3 cups whole-wheat couscous

Instructions

1. In a large pot over medium heat, sauté onion, green bell pepper, and red bell pepper in olive oil for 5 to 7 minutes or until softened. Add garlic, curry powder, cumin, coriander, cinnamon, 1 1/2 teaspoon sea salt, and 1/2 teaspoon black pepper and sauté for 2 more minutes. Add sweet potato and sauté for 5 more minutes. Add and combine zucchini, chickpeas, diced tomatoes, 1/2 cup vegetable stock, and 2 tablespoons lemon juice. Cover, reduce heat to low, and simmer 15 to 20 minutes, or until vegetables are tender.

2. In a medium saucepan, combine the remaining 4 1/2 cups vegetable stock and 4 tablespoons lemon juice and bring to a boil over high heat. Add couscous, remaining 1 1/2 teaspoon sea salt, remaining 1/2 teaspoon black pepper, and stir to combine. Cover, remove from heat, and set aside for 5 minutes. Remove lid and fluff couscous with a fork. Serve stew over couscous.

Deliciously Easy Penne

SERVINGS: 8
PREP TIME: 10 min.
TOTAL TIME: 35 min.

Ingredients

- 1 (16 ounce) package penne pasta
- 2 tablespoons olive oil
- 1/4 cup chopped red onion
- 1 tablespoon chopped garlic
- 1/4 cup white wine
- 2 (14.5 ounce) cans diced tomatoes
- 1 cup grated Parmesan cheese

Instructions

1. Bring a large pot of lightly salted water to boil. Add pasta and cook for 8 to 10 minutes or until al dente. Drain.
2. Heat oil in a skillet over medium heat. Stir in onion and garlic, and cook until tender. Add and mix in wine and tomatoes. Cook for 10 minutes, stirring occasionally.
3. Toss with pasta and top with Parmesan cheese. Serve.

Moroccan Roasted Vegetables

SERVINGS: 4
PREP TIME: 10 min.
TOTAL TIME: 50 min.

Ingredients

- 1 onion, cut into 1/4 inch thick slices
- 1 zucchini, cut into 1/4 inch thick semicircles
- 1 eggplant, cut into 1/2 inch thick semicircles
- 1 sweet potato, peeled and cut into 1/4-inch thick semicircles
- 1 red pepper, cut into 1/4-inch strips
- 2 tomatoes, chopped
- 1 can (15.5 ounces) or 1 1/2 cups cooked chickpeas, drained
- 3 garlic cloves, minced or pressed
- 2 tablespoons vegetable oil
- 1 tablespoon fresh lemon juice
- 1 tablespoon ground cumin
- 1 1/2 teaspoons turmeric
- 1 1/2 teaspoons ground cinnamon
- 1 1/2 teaspoons paprika
- 1/4 teaspoon cayenne
- 2 teaspoons salt

Instructions

1. Preheat oven to 400°F (200°C).
2. In a large bowl, combine all the ingredients and mix well.
3. Spread vegetables onto an 11 x 17 inch baking tray and place in oven for 20 minutes. Stir well and bake for another 20 minutes or until the vegetables are tender.

Greek-Style Potatoes

SERVINGS: 4
PREP TIME: 10 min.
TOTAL TIME: 2 hours

Ingredients

- 1/3 cup olive oil
- 1 1/2 cups water
- 2 cloves garlic, finely chopped
- 1/4 cup lemon juice
- 1 teaspoon dried thyme
- 1 teaspoon dried rosemary
- ground black pepper, to taste
- 6 potatoes, peeled and quartered

Instructions

1. Preheat oven to 350°F (175°C).
2. Mix olive oil, water, garlic, lemon juice, thyme, rosemary, bouillon cubes and pepper in a small bowl.
3. Place potatoes evenly in a medium baking dish. Pour mixture over the potatoes. Cover and bake 1 1/2 to 2 hours in the oven. Turn occasionally until tender.

Mediterranean Vegan Flounder

SERVINGS: 4
PREP TIME: 15 min.
TOTAL TIME: 45 min.

Ingredients

- 5 Roma (plum) tomatoes
- 2 tablespoons extra virgin olive oil
- 1/2 Spanish onion, chopped
- 2 cloves garlic, chopped
- 1 pinch Italian seasoning
- 24 Kalamata olives, pitted and chopped
- 1/4 cup white wine
- 1/4 cup capers
- 1 teaspoon fresh lemon juice
- 6 leaves fresh basil, chopped
- 3 tablespoons freshly grated Parmesan cheese
- 1 pound vegan fish fillets
- 6 leaves fresh basil, torn

Instructions

1. Preheat oven to 425°F (220°C).
2. Bring a saucepan of water to a boil. Place tomatoes into the boiling water and remove immediately into a medium bowl of ice water. Drain. Remove and discard tomato skins. Chop tomatoes and set aside.
3. Heat oil in a skillet over medium heat. Sauté onion about 5 minutes or until tender. Stir in tomatoes, garlic and Italian seasoning and cook 5 to 7 minutes or until tomatoes are tender. Mix in olives, wine, capers, lemon juice, and 1/2 the basil. Reduce heat, blend in Parmesan cheese, and cook about 15 minutes or until sauce is thick.
4. Place vegan fish fillets in a shallow baking dish. Pour sauce over fillets and top with the rest of the basil leaves.
5. Bake 12 minutes in the oven or until vegan fillets are heated through.

Chickpeas and Spinach

SERVINGS: 4
PREP TIME: 15 min.
TOTAL TIME: 25 min.

Ingredients

- 1 tablespoon extra-virgin olive oil
- 4 cloves garlic, minced
- 1/2 onion, diced
- 1 (10 ounce) box frozen chopped spinach, thawed and drained well
- 1 (12 ounce) can garbanzo beans (chickpeas), drained
- 1/2 teaspoon cumin
- 1/2 teaspoon salt

Instructions

1. Heat olive oil over medium-low heat in a skillet. Cook garlic and onion in the oil about 5 minutes or until translucent. Stir in the spinach, garbanzo beans (chickpeas), cumin, and salt.
2. As the mixture cooks, lightly mash the chickpeas with the spoon. Cook until thoroughly heated.

Grilled Mediterranean Vegetable Sandwich

SERVINGS: 6
PREP/TOTAL TIME: 40 min. + sitting

Ingredients

- 1 eggplant, sliced into strips
- 2 red bell peppers
- 2 tablespoons olive oil
- 2 Portobello mushrooms, sliced
- 3 cloves garlic, crushed
- 4 tablespoons mayonnaise
- 1 (1 pound) loaf focaccia bread

Instructions

1. Preheat oven to 400°F (200°C).
2. Brush eggplant and red bell peppers all over with 1 tablespoon olive oil. Place on a baking sheet and roast in oven for about 25 minutes or until tender. Remove and set aside to cool.
3. Heat 1 tablespoon of olive oil, add and stir mushrooms until tender.
4. Stir crushed garlic into mayonnaise. Slice focaccia in half lengthwise and spread mayonnaise mix on one or both halves.
5. Cool peppers and then peel, core, and slice. Arrange eggplant, peppers and mushrooms on focaccia. Wrap sandwich in plastic wrap and place a cutting board on top. Place a few heavy items on cutting board to weigh it down.
6. Allow sandwich to sit for 2 hours.
7. Slice and serve.

Saffron Risotto with Broccoli

SERVINGS: 4
PREP/ TOTAL TIME: 45 min.

Ingredients

- 3 cups vegetable stock
- 4 cups small broccoli florets
- 1/4 teaspoon Spanish saffron, divided
- 1 tablespoon olive oil
- 1 medium leek (1 1/2 cups), white and pale green part halved and thinly sliced
- 3/4 cup Arborio rice

Instructions

1. In medium saucepan, bring vegetable stock to a simmer. Add broccoli, and cook 2 to 3 minutes, or until tender but crisp. Remove florets from broth and set aside. Stir 1/8 teaspoon saffron into hot broth, reduce heat to low or turn off. Cover and keep hot.
2. Heat oil in saucepan over medium heat. Add leek, and sauté 3 to 5 minutes, or until tender. Stir in rice and sauté 3 to 5 minutes, or until rice is opaque.
3. Reduce heat to medium-low and stir in 1 cup stock. Cook rice until liquid is mostly absorbed, and stir frequently. Continually add stock 1/2 cup at a time, about 10 minutes, stirring until liquid is absorbed. Stir in remaining 1/8 teaspoon saffron before adding last of stock. Cook until liquid is mostly absorbed. Remove from heat, and stir in broccoli. Cover risotto, and let stand 2 to 3 minutes or until broccoli is hot.
4. Season with salt and pepper. Serve.

Greek Pizzas

SERVINGS: 6
PREP TIME: 10 min.
TOTAL TIME: 35 min.

Ingredients

- 6 five-inch of your favorite pizza dough
- 1 package spinach dip mix
- 1 1/2 cups yogurt
- 4 ounces feta cheese
- 2 ounces diced black olives
- 1 cup diced tomatoes
- 1/2 cup sliced red onions
- 1 1/2 teaspoons fresh peppermint leaves

Instructions

1. Pre-bake dough for 10 minutes at 350°F (177°C), and set aside.
2. Combine spinach dip mix and yogurt in a medium mixing bowl. Spread mixture on partially baked crusts. Sprinkle each crust with feta cheese, diced olives, diced tomatoes, sliced onions and peppermint leaves.
3. Return crusts to oven and bake for 10 to 15 minutes or until golden brown.

Spinach, Cherry Tomato, and Pepper Penne Rigate

SERVINGS: 4
PREP/TOTAL TIME: 30 min.

Ingredients

- 2 1/2 cups penne Rigate pasta
- 1 tablespoon olive oil
- 2 cloves (2 teaspoon)garlic, minced
- 1 (12 ounces) jar roasted red peppers, rinsed, drained, patted dry, and sliced
- 10 ounces cherry tomatoes, halved
- 4 cups packed baby spinach leaves
- 1/4 cup chopped pitted Kalamata olives
- 1 tablespoon finely chopped fresh oregano
- 1 1/2 teaspoon grated lemon zest
- 1/4 teaspoon freshly ground black pepper

Instructions

1. Prepare pasta according to directions on package. Drain and reserve 1/2 cup pasta water.
2. Heat oil over medium heat in large nonstick skillet. Add garlic, cook 1 minute or until lightly browned, while frequently stirring.
3. Add roasted peppers, increase heat to high, and cook 3 to 4 minutes or until lightly browned, stirring occasionally.
4. Add tomatoes, spinach, olives, oregano, lemon zest, and pepper. Cook 4 to 6 minutes, or until vegetables soften, stirring frequently. Add pasta and reserved pasta-cooking water. Cover and cook 3 more minutes, or until heated through.

Cilantro Pesto

SERVINGS: 8
PREP TIME: 15 min.
TOTAL TIME: 30 min.

Ingredients

- 1 (16 ounce) package farfalle pasta
- 1 bunch fresh cilantro
- 5 cloves garlic, minced
- 1 tablespoon white wine vinegar
- 1/4 cup grated Parmesan cheese
- 1/2 teaspoon cayenne pepper
- 1/2 cup walnuts or pecans
- salt to taste
- 1/2 cup olive oil

Instructions

1. Bring a large pot of salted water to a boil. Add pasta and cook for 8 to 10 minutes or until al dente. Drain.
2. In a food processor or blender, combine cilantro, garlic, vinegar, Parmesan cheese, cayenne pepper, nuts, and salt. Add 1/4 cup of the olive oil, and blend. Add more olive oil until the pesto reaches desired consistency.
3. Pour pesto in a small saucepan and warm over low heat, stirring constantly, until simmering. Pour and toss over cooked pasta.

Toasted Quinoa Tabbouleh

SERVINGS: 6
PREP TIME: 15 min.
TOTAL TIME: 45 min.

Ingredients

- 1 1/2 cups quinoa
- 1 3/4 teaspoon fine sea salt
- 1/3 cup olive oil
- 3/4 cup lemon juice (about 4 small lemons)
- 2 cloves garlic (about 2 teaspoon), minced
- 1/2 tsp. freshly ground black pepper
- 2 cups diced tomatoes or quartered cherry tomatoes
- 1 1/2 cups parsley, chopped
- 3 unpeeled Persian cucumbers(about 1 1/3 cups), diced
- 4 green onions (about 1 cup), thinly sliced
- 1/2 cup fresh mint leaves, chopped

Instructions

1. Rinse quinoa in a strainer under running water and drain.
2. Heat large skillet over medium heat. Add quinoa and cook 10 minutes or until moisture evaporates and quinoa is golden and fragrant. Stir constantly.
3. In saucepan, bring 2 1/2 cups water to boil. Add 1/4 teaspoon of salt and quinoa. Return to a boil, reduce heat to medium-low, and cover. Simmer 20 minutes, or until quinoa is tender and liquid has absorbed. Fluff quinoa with a fork, and transfer to large bowl. Allow to cool.
4. Whisk oil, lemon juice, garlic, pepper, and remaining 1 1/2 teaspoon of salt in small bowl. Stir tomatoes, parsley, cucumbers, green onions, and mint into quinoa. Pour dressing on top and toss to coat.
5. Serve at room temperature, or refrigerate and cover until cooled.

Jackfruit Gyros

SERVINGS: 4
PREP TIME: 10 min.
TOTAL TIME: 50 min.

Ingredients

- 1 tablespoon vegan or regular margarine
- 1 large onion, halved and thinly sliced
- 1 (20 oz.) can young jackfruit in brine, rinsed, drained, and shredded
- 3/4 cup low-sodium vegetable broth
- 4 tablespoon lemon juice
- 2 teaspoon dried oregano
- 1 teaspoon low-sodium soy sauce
- 3/4 teaspoon ground coriander

Instructions

1. Heat margarine in a skillet over medium heat until sizzling. Add onion and sauté 3 to 4 minutes or until softened. Add jackfruit and cook 20 minutes, or until brown and caramelized.
2. Add broth, 2 tablespoons lemon juice, oregano, soy sauce, and coriander, and season with salt and pepper. Simmer 10 to 15 minutes, or until liquid has evaporated.
3. Stir in remaining 2 tablespoons lemon juice.

Stuffed Grape Leaves Casserole

SERVINGS: 8
PREP TIME: 15 min.
TOTAL TIME: 1 1/2 hour

Ingredients

- 30 fresh or jarred grape leaves
- 2 or 3 tablespoons olive oil
- 1 large onion, finely diced
- 1 cup brown rice
- 2 cups low-sodium tomato or vegetable juice
- 1 cup chopped unsalted, hulled pistachios
- 1 cup chopped fresh parsley
- 1 cup chopped fresh mint
- 1 cup raisins or dried currants
- 1/4 cup lemon juice
- 1 lemon, sliced, for garnish
- Pomegranate molasses, optional

Instructions

1. Dip grape leaves in large pot of boiling water 2 minutes. Drain and set aside.
2. Heat oil over medium heat in large saucepan. Add onion and sauté 7 to 10 minutes, or until starting to brown. Add rice and 2 1/2 cups of water and bring to a boil. Reduce heat to medium-low and cover. Cook 30 to 40 minutes or until liquid absorbs. Remove from heat, and stir in tomato juice, pistachios, parsley, mint, raisins, and lemon juice. Season with salt and pepper.
3. Preheat oven to 350°F (175°C).
4. Brush 2 quart baking dish with olive oil. Pat grape leaves dry. Line the bottom and side of baking dish with grape leaves. Letting leaves hang over sides. Spread half of rice mix over grape leaves. Top with more grape leaves and top with remaining rice mix. Cover with remaining grape leaves and fold over grape leaves around edges. Brush top with oil. Bake for 30 to 40 minutes or until grape leaves on top darken and casserole is dry and firm.

5. Dip knife in cold water and cut to make 8 servings. Remove servings with spatula and garnish with lemon slices. Drizzle with pomegranate molasses, if desired.

Muhammara

SERVINGS: 6
PREP/ TOTAL TIME: 1 hour 30 min.

Ingredients

- 2 cups walnuts
- 3 large red bell peppers
- 4 tablespoons olive oil, divided
- 4 cloves garlic, sliced
- 2 teaspoon salt
- 2 tablespoons pomegranate syrup

Instructions

2. Preheat oven to 375°F (190°C).
3. Place walnuts on baking sheet, and bake for 10 to 12 minutes, or until fragrant and lightly browned. Allow to cool.
4. On a separate baking sheet, place bell peppers and roast in oven for 1 hour, or until skins are black. Turn occasionally. Transfer peppers to bowl, and cover with plate and cool for 15 minutes. Rub off blackened skins and remove seeds.
5. In small skillet over medium heat, cook 2 tablespoons of olive oil. Add garlic and sauté 1 minute. Remove from heat and let the garlic and oil cool.
6. In a blender, purée bell peppers, walnuts, garlic, remaining olive oil, salt, and pomegranate syrup until smooth. Season with salt and pepper. Transfer to small bowl and serve.

Gorgonzola, Fig & Spinach Pizza

SERVINGS: 2-4
PREP TIME: 15 min. + setting
TOTAL TIME: 45 min.

Ingredients

- 1/2 cup brown rice flour
- 1/2 cup chickpea flour
- 1/2 cup potato starch
- 1 tablespoon sugar
- 3 teaspoons yeast, divided
- 2 teaspoons guar gum or xanthan gum
- 3/4 teaspoon salt
- 2 egg whites
- 2 tablespoons olive oil
- 4 ounces (114 g) Gorgonzola cheese
- 1/4 cup fat-free milk
- 3 cups baby spinach leaves
- 6 fresh or dried figs, quartered
- 2 tablespoons pine nuts
- 3 tablespoons dry-cured, pitted black olives, optional

Instructions

1. Preheat oven to 400°F (200°C).
2. In a bowl, whisk brown rice flour, chickpea flour, potato starch, and sugar. In a separate bowl scoop 1/2 cup flour mixture. Add and mix in 1 teaspoon of yeast and 1/2 cup warm water. Cover with plastic wrap and let set in a warm place for 4 to 12 hours or until bubbly and fragrant.
3. Whisk remaining 2 teaspoon of yeast, guar gum, and salt in dry flour mixture. Stir egg whites and 3/4 cup warm water into wet yeast-flour mix. Combine and mix wet mixture into dry mixture until there are no lumps. Stir in oil. Cover and place in warm place for 20 minutes or until it rises. Place dough onto pizza pan and press dough flat.

4. In a blender or food processor, purée cheese and milk until smooth. Spread cheese mixture on the dough. Top with spinach, figs, pine nuts, and olives.
5. Place pizza on rack in oven, and bake 20 to 25 minutes, or until crust is browned and crisp on bottom. Let stand 5 minutes.
6. Slice and serve.

Potato and Pesto Frittata

SERVINGS: 8
PREP TIME: 15 min.
TOTAL TIME: 1 hour

Ingredients

* 3 tablespoons olive oil, divided
* 1 1/2 lbs. (3 cups) red potatoes, cubed
* 1 small onion (1 cup), diced
* 1 small red bell pepper (1 cup), diced
* 2 cups fresh basil leaves, parsley leaves, arugula, or watercress
* 2 cloves garlic, peeled
* 2 tablespoons Dijon mustard
* 2 tablespoons all-purpose flour
* 6 large eggs
* 3 large egg whites
* 1/4 cup grated Parmesan cheese

Instructions

1. Heat 1 tablespoon oil over medium heat in a nonstick skillet. Add potatoes, onion, and bell pepper, and cook 15 minutes, or until potatoes and onion start to brown, stirring often. Transfer potato mixture to a large bowl. Season with salt and pepper and cool 10 minutes.
2. Place basil and garlic in food processor and pulse until finely chopped. Add flour and mustard, and pulse until combined. Add eggs, egg whites, and Parmesan cheese and blend for one minute, or until foamy. Combine egg mixture with potato mixture.
3. Heat 2 tablespoons of oil in nonstick skillet over medium-low heat. Spread potato-egg mixture evenly into hot skillet. Cover, and cook 10 minutes. Lift bottom and sides of frittata with spatula so uncooked egg mixture reaches the pan. Cover and cook 10 minutes, or until brown and crispy on bottom and sides.
4. Remove skillet from heat, loosen frittata edge, and place large plate over skillet. Invert frittata onto plate and slide back into skillet uncooked-side down. Cover and cook 5 minutes, or until both sides

are crispy and brown. Transfer to serving plate and cool. Serve at room temperature.

Roasted Red Pepper Crostini with Balsamic Vinegar

SERVINGS: 6
PREP TIME: 15 min.
TOTAL TIME: 1 hour 15 min.

Ingredients

- 3 large red bell peppers
- 3 tablespoons pine nuts
- 1 red jalapeño chili
- 3 teaspoon olive oil, divided
- 1 1/2 tablespoons chopped fresh parsley
- 1 1/2 tablespoons chopped fresh mint
- 3 cloves (1 tablespoon) garlic, minced
- 1 whole garlic clove, peeled, divided
- 1/2 cup balsamic vinegar
- 1 tablespoon agave syrup
- 6 1/3 inch-thick slices ciabatta bread, toasted

Instructions

1. Heat pine nuts in skillet over medium heat for 3 to 4 minutes, or until brown, constantly shaking the pan. Set aside.
2. Place oven rack in highest position and preheat broiler. Coat bell peppers and jalapeño with 1 teaspoon oil. Place on baking sheet, and broil 15 minutes, turning often, until blistered and partly blacked on all sides. Transfer to bowl, cover, and cool. Peel, seed, slice bell peppers into thin strips; finely chop jalapeños; and transfer to bowl. Add pine nuts, parsley, mint, minced garlic, and remaining 2 teaspoon oil, tossing to combine. Season with black pepper.
3. In a small saucepan, simmer vinegar and agave syrup over medium heat. Cook for 10 minutes, stirring occasionally, until mixture reduces to about 3 tablespoons and coats pan bottom when tilted. Stir 1 tablespoon balsamic syrup into roasted pepper mixture. Marinate roasted pepper mixture 30 minutes or chill overnight. Top

bread slices with roasted pepper mixture, and drizzle with remaining balsamic reduction.

Cauliflower and Paprika Pita Pockets

Ingredients

- 1 head cauliflower, cut into bite-size florets
- 3 tablespoons olive oil
- 2 tablespoons sweet Hungarian paprika
- 1/2 teaspoon ground black pepper
- 1/2 teaspoon fine sea salt
- 1 small red onion, diced
- 1 clove garlic (1 teaspoon), minced
- 1/2 cup low-sodium vegetable broth
- 2 tablespoons lemon juice
- 4 pita bread rounds, halved and warmed

Instructions

1. Add 1 inch of water to a pan and insert a steamer basket or colander. Add an inch or two of water. The water surface should be just under the basket. Pour out some water if necessary. Bring the water to a boil over high heat. Add and steam cauliflower for 7 to 9 minutes, or until tender.
2. In a nonstick skillet over medium-low heat, cook oil, paprika, pepper, and salt for 2 minutes, or until fragrant, constantly stirring. Add onion and garlic, and sauté 2 minutes. Stir in broth and cauliflower, simmering for 3 minutes. Remove from heat, and stir in lemon juice.
3. Serve with pita halves.

Spelt Olive Loaf

SERVINGS: 2
PREP TIME: 20 min. + rising + cooling
TOTAL TIME: 3 hours

Ingredients

- 2 tablespoons honey
- 1 (0.25 oz.) package active dry yeast
- 1/2 cup olive oil
- 2 tablespoons salt
- 8 cups spelt bread flour
- 1 cup pitted black olives, sliced

Instructions

1. In a bowl, combine honey, yeast, and 2 cups of warm water. Let stand 10 minutes, or until yeast becomes foamy. Add oil and salt. Stir in flour 1 cup at a time until a ball is formed.
2. Place dough on floured surface, sprinkle with flour. Knead 15 minutes, or until dough is smooth and no longer sticks to hands, adding flour as needed.
3. Transfer the dough to a lightly oiled bowl. Cover with moist towel, and let rise for an hour or until he dough doubles in size. Punch down dough, and let rise another hour or refrigerate overnight.
4. Spray two baking sheets with cooking spray or line with parchment paper. Place dough on floured work surface and knead in olives. Form into 2 round loaves and stretch the surface until smooth, drawing excess dough at bottom. Pinch a seam at bottom of dough. Place on prepared baking sheets and cover with moist towel. Let rise 30 minutes or until doubled in size.
5. Preheat oven to 400°F (200°C) and bake loaves for 45 to 50 minutes, or until browned. Cool 20 minutes and serve.

Mediterranean Pressed Sandwich

SERVINGS: 6
PREP/TOTAL TIME: 20 min. + refrigeration

Ingredients

- 1 small eggplant, cut lengthwise in 1/4-inch slices
- 1 small zucchini, cut lengthwise in 1/4-inch slices
- 1 small yellow squash, cut lengthwise in 1/4-inch slices
- 3 tablespoons olive oil, divided
- 1 large loaf ciabatta bread, halved
- 1/3 cup prepared pesto
- 1/3 cup prepared tapenade
- 2 jarred roasted red peppers, sliced
- 1 (8 oz.) pkg. fresh mozzarella, drained and sliced
- 2 tablespoons balsamic vinegar

Instructions

1. Heat grill pan on medium-high heat. Brush eggplant, zucchini, and yellow squash with 2 tablespoons of olive oil. Place on pan and grill 3 to 4 minutes on each side, or until softened and charred. Transfer to a plate.
2. Hollow inside of bread and spread pesto inside one side. Spread tapenade on other side.
3. Inside the bread, layer eggplant, zucchini, yellow squash, roasted red peppers, and mozzarella on one side. Drizzle with balsamic vinegar and remaining olive oil. Season with salt and pepper.
4. Press and wrap sandwich tightly in plastic wrap. Place on baking sheet and weigh down with two large cans or another heavy item.
5. Refrigerate 2 hours or overnight. Unwrap, slice, and serve.

THANK YOU

Thank you for checking out my Vegetarian Mediterranean Cookbook. I hope you enjoyed these recipes as much as I have. I am always looking for feedback on how to improve, so if you have any questions, suggestions, or comments please send me an email at susan.evans.author@gmail.com. Also, if you enjoyed the book would you consider leaving on honest review? As a new author, they help me out in a big way. Thanks again, and have fun cooking!

Other popular books by Susan Evans

Quick & Easy Asian Vegetarian Cookbook:
Over 50 recipes for stir fries, rice, noodles, and appetizers

Vegetarian Slow Cooker Cookbook:
Over 75 recipes for meals, soups, stews, desserts, and sides

Quick & Easy Vegetarian Rice Cooker Meals:
Over 50 recipes for breakfast, main dishes, and desserts

Quick & Easy Vegan Desserts Cookbook:
Over 80 delicious recipes for cakes, cupcakes, brownies, cookies, fudge,
pies, candy, and so much more!

Quick & Easy Rice Cooker Meals:
Over 60 recipes for breakfast, main dishes, soups, and desserts

Quick & Easy Microwave Meals:
Over 50 recipes for breakfast, snacks, meals and desserts

Halloween Cookbook:
80 Ghoulish recipes for appetizers, meals, drinks, and desserts

Printed in Great Britain
by Amazon